SENSELESS UNHAPPINESS

My Marital Testimony

Ronald L. Wren.

Website: leveragexpress.com

Contact information: leveragexm@gmail.com

ISBN: 979-8-9930868-0-4 (Paperback)
ISBN: 979-8-9930868-1-1 (Hardcover)
ISBN: 979-8-9930868-2-8 (E.BOOK)

Book design by Designer. Mercy E. (Fiverr)

The workbook is a practical, faith-based guide for couples to reflect, communicate, and take actionable steps toward healing and strengthening their marriage. It combines introspective questions, exercises, and biblical principles to foster growth, reconciliation, and deeper connection. Kolbaba Ginger. "Just Say Yes for a Happier Marriage." *Focus on the Family,* 2018. In *10 Simple Ideas for a Happier Marriage,* posted at

https://www.focusonthefamily.com/marriage/10-simple-ideas-for-a-happier-marriage2/

Yerkovich, Kay, and Milan Yerkovich. "How childhood experiences impact love styles: Five unhealthy love styles." *Focus on the Family Australia,* 2012. Available at;

https://families.org.au/article/how-childhood-experiences-impact-love-styles/ Focus on the Family Australia

Dr. Myles Munroe, "The Purpose and Power of Love and Marriage" (2005)

Contents

Forward

Ron Wren writes with a fire that cannot be ignored. In Senseless Unhappiness, he opens his heart and shares the raw journey of moving from hopeless to hopeful. With honesty and passion, Ron invites men and women to step into their identity as overcomers, breaking free from the chains of life's circumstances.

The book's powerful theme, Rescue, Renew, Revive, Reconcile, is more than a framework; it's a spiritual roadmap. Each chapter carries the reader through a shift from darkness into light, offering hope where despair once lived. Ron's testimony is not just his own story, but a call to transformation for anyone ready to embrace freedom and purpose.

If you are searching for a resource that speaks to the heart, ignites courage, and awakens spiritual clarity, Senseless Unhappiness is a must-read. It is a book that doesn't just inform, it revives.

Pastor Sandy Burkett, Ph.D., has been a full-time pastoral counselor since 1980. She has a Ph.D. in Biblical Counseling from Trinity Theological Seminary. Her Ph.D. research was on the Restoration of Joy in Victims of Childhood Trauma.

Dr. Sandy is a sought-after speaker and minister. She is published and has presented papers at the American Association of Christian Counselors and special conferences on Dissociative Identity Disorder. She teaches or co-teaches many workshops and conferences.

– Dr. Sandy Burkett

Introduction

I began writing on my iPad to cope with the frustrations of my second marriage. The perpetual pattern of my "senseless unhappiness" began to solidify by the third year of marriage. Writing became my therapy and developed into an intentional focus to keep my sanity, somewhere around the sixth year of marriage. I wrote to try and gather my thoughts. Though sporadic at times, it became a regular practice. I began to realize that what I was writing could help other couples. I would purposely focus on an introspective, solutions-oriented approach. Through trial and error, I learned that complaining to others (including family and acquaintances did not help at all. There were times before I began writing, when I would all too often talk to myself in my car when I was alone; of course, that was not the best therapy.

My wife and I went to a few Counseling sessions, but not enough to effect the change we needed. Writing has helped bring clarity, even though it has not brought the change in my everyday marriage that we so badly needed.

Who is this book for?

Your marriage is doing fine, so the book is not for you. Please do not read.

Give it to someone else who is having issues; However, if you have considered divorcing or separating from your spouse within the past few months to 5 years. This book is also for those who find themselves single and divorced. If you are currently separated from your spouse, if you are in constant upheaval in your relationship, and if you live in the same house but sleep in separate rooms. This Book is for YOU! If you are considering leaving your spouse, but do not dare to do so, this book is for you. Suppose you do not like where your marriage is or its status. This book is for you. If you have given up on your marriage, this book is for you. If you are at the End of your rope, this book is for you. If you tried marital counseling, but it has not worked, this book is for you. I think you get the gist.

You may find parts of my testimony relatable; some parts might make you laugh or cry.

My prayer is that, once you're done reading this, my story, you will make the changes necessary to make all YHWH has created for your marital bliss a reality.

Sharing My Story

I often wondered whether it truly mattered if others knew my personal story. On its own, perhaps it isn't important. However, I came to realize that the real value lies in the possibility that sharing my experiences might help someone else face similar struggles. That is where the true importance rests, not in seeking to make someone else look bad or to present myself in a favorable light, but in being honest for the sake of healing.

Choosing vulnerability is never easy. When someone finally musters the courage to open and share their pain, it can be devastating to be dismissed or shut down by others. That rejection feels like a gut punch, especially when only you and God know your true intentions. Even if others misunderstand or question your motives, there comes a point where you must decide: will you stay silent to please others, or will you speak your truth and risk vulnerability, knowing you might regret staying quiet about the pain you have endured?

Scripture reminds us in James 5:16, "Confess your faults one to the other that you may be healed." Sharing our struggles is not just about being heard; it is about creating the possibility for healing, both for ourselves and for others who may be suffering in silence. This is my marital testimony, an alarming siren that calls for the help your troubled marriage needs. Stop ignoring the prominent warnings.

<u>Disclaimer:</u> The content of this book is provided for informational purposes only. While every effort has been made to ensure the accuracy and completeness of the information contained herein, the author makes no representations or warranties of any kind, express or implied, about the completeness, accuracy, reliability, suitability, or availability with respect to the book or the information, products, services, or related graphics contained in the book for any purpose.

Any reliance you place on such information is therefore strictly at your own risk. The author shall not be liable for any loss or damage, including, without limitation, indirect or consequential loss or damage, or any loss or damage whatsoever arising from the use of this book.

The views and opinions expressed in this book are those of the author and do not necessarily reflect the official policy or position of any other individual, agency, organization, employer, or company. Any resemblance to actual people, living or dead, or actual events is purely coincidental.

This book is not intended to provide professional advice, including but not limited to legal, medical, financial, or other professional services. Readers should consult appropriate professionals for specific advice tailored to their individual circumstances.

Comments

I must commend you for such an amazing piece of work. My Marital Testimony truly spoke to me on a personal level; it felt as though it was written just for me. As a freelancer, my schedule often keeps me so busy that I don't always give my marriage the attention it deserves. Reading your story, with its honesty, vulnerability, and faith-filled insights, has opened my eyes in many ways. It reminded me that I am not alone in these struggles, and that intentional effort, prayer, and perspective can make all the difference. Your words have deeply impacted me, and I am grateful that you chose to share your testimony. It is not just a book; it is a guide, a mirror, and an encouragement to anyone who desires to build a stronger marriage despite life's challenges. The honesty and openness you shared drew me in and made it feel so personal, as though it were written for me. The balance between your story, the lessons, and the faith insights is perfect. It's real, it's relatable, and it gives me hope.

Thank you so much! Mercy E.

Work Book summary

Insights on Marriage and Spiritual Authority

The author provides insights into the spiritual aspects of marriage and the importance of submission.

- He outlines key principles for a successful marriage, including submission, unity, and intimacy.
- The author stresses the significance of understanding spiritual authority as designed by God.
- He encourages couples to align their lives with biblical principles to strengthen their marriage.

SENSELESS UNHAPPINESS

My Marital Testimony

Chapter 1
It makes no Sense

I chose Senseless Unhappiness (SU) as a title for those of us who have been in or are currently in a marriage that is on life support. It appears the marriage is in disrepair. Different circumstances may lead a couple to what I have labelled Senseless Unhappiness (SU); however, the result is the same. When one or both of you highly consider giving up on marriage and are close to the brink of divorce, fill in your status of Senseless Unhappiness (SU)... You stay together and put on the charade as if all is well. Senselessness can affect parts or the whole of a marriage, intimacy, child rearing, upkeep of our home, hygiene, the financial climate of our home, and more. Mental wholeness is affected, and stress weighs heavily on your well-being, including your dietary practices, exercise, hobbies, activities, and social interaction.

Senseless unhappiness breeds senseless depravity, senseless sadness, senseless poverty, senseless loss, senseless pain, senseless remorse. Senseless unhappiness is when you momentarily consider other things that will make your senseless unhappiness even more senseless. Those who are oblivious to this have lost their sensitivity to the Holy Spirit. Often, we spiral off into a tangent, taking us further into unhappiness. I know in the Christian world, we say God does not promise happiness. Please don't get this mixed up; happiness is still something worth having. I won't spend a lot of time on that because I do know the difference between happiness and joy. Joy is what I choose to have and what I know I have in Christ. As it is written concerning Christ Jesus, *"He endured the cross and despised the shame for the joy that was set before Him." Hebrews 12:2*

Senseless unhappiness (SU) is the experience of deep discontent in a marriage when, on the surface, there seems to be no obvious reason for it. It is the weight of frustration, bitterness, and emotional distance that settles in, even though you still love your spouse. It is the unsettling reality of feeling ill regard toward someone you care about deeply. You may cry out for help internally, yet feel as though no one truly understands or can intervene.

This kind of unhappiness often emerges in seasons of marital disharmony, regardless of how long the marriage has lasted. It can persist even after a meaningful church service, a powerful prayer time, or a sermon that speaks directly to your heart. Outwardly, everything appears spiritually aligned, yet inwardly, the discontent remains. Senseless unhappiness is the painful contradiction of knowing you "should" feel peace, yet finding that peace absent.

Be careful with the ears you reveal your business to, marital and otherwise. I discovered after a while that the feedback received from others was not from a healthy place for my marriage. I was so frustrated by some of the input I received. I made a vow to myself that I would only take my problems to the Lord and be patient to hear His instruction. Bad advice from family members or friends, most of the time, makes things worse. I also realized that I would not receive bad advice from others if I never revealed my problems to them. No one can fix your unhappiness, not even a professional. Most times, others treat your problem with something so off base that it leaves you shaking your Head.

Senseless unhappiness (SU) is when the solution is obvious but not realized. Senseless unhappiness (SU) is when you know the Lord, you know the biblical answers, you know His Word concerning the situation, yet the situation remains unchanged. You can only control yourself, not your mate. Senseless unhappiness (SU) is when godly principles are not lived out in your marriage. So, you find yourself stuck and unhappy.

You are in what I have labeled as the going through process, the phase of going through, in the strain of the process. Praising your way through a particular thing is feasible for a moment; what you do is just that: praise your way through. Get lost in work or a hobby. Others focus on their children, other family matters, and friends. The reality is that the problem still exists and has not changed. You're stuck in go-through mode. You believe you have done all you know to do to move forward. The reality is that the bulk of the problem is not being addressed. People tend to stick their heads in the sand, hoping things will get better. Instead, we're tempted to settle for shallow fixes rather than concrete solutions.

Praising God keeps me mentally stable and serves my spirit man, helping me focus on my current circumstances. My inner thoughts are going off like a blaring alarm; my marriage is on tilt. Some individuals find themselves wondering what happened to the playful flirting exchanges once shared with their mate. Like, I cannot wait to get home and kiss you and make Love to you. Remember the excitement of going out on a date? The sentimental exchange of text throughout a given day. This kind of thing makes a person scream, "What the cracky HAPPEN?" (Disclaimer: I'm not justifying cussing, but I admit I've wanted to many times in the throes of SU). Despite my Love for my wife, I wanted to avoid another horrible argument with her; after all, I still deeply cared for her.

When my late wife and I got married, she had just turned forty, which was a couple of weeks after our wedding. I turned 52 a month or so after we married. Our marriage was a second for us both. Her first marriage lasted 5 years, and mine lasted 25 years. The reasons for our marriage's ending were vastly different. I fathered a daughter before my first marriage and was a father to three boys from my first marriage. I was also a grandparent a few times over. My wife was born and raised in Brooklyn, NY; she was the youngest of 5, and she had a twin brother. She was a college grad and received an associate's degree. She ended up in Columbus, Ohio, and became a member of a Church there. My wife was raising two boys as a single mom, a six-year-old and a nine-year-old.

I grew up in Cleveland, Ohio; I was the second oldest of 5. I attended Ohio State after graduating from High School. I attend College at Ohio State University (OSU). College ended before the end of my second year. I went into the work world. I became a Christian in 1980. I answered a call to the Ministry. I ended up in Atlanta for work, and I served as an Associate Minister for 6 years. Another major shift happened in my life, and I moved back to Columbus to answer a call to become a Pastor, but that opportunity did not work out. My first marriage was not in a good place. I divorced my first wife after 25 years.

My wife and I met at Church. We were two good-looking people, in my biased opinion, who fell in Love.

I clearly recall her scooting next to me on her couch during the early times of our dating. She made the first move to kiss me, that giggle of hers, her warm hands, her lying on my chest, snuggling close, even making me shy and skittish. Her words of longing and expressions of desire for me, the feeling that this all is so wonderful, an unbelievable feeling of Love. Initially, we settled in nicely. She was genuinely kind in a way I had never experienced before. She doted on me so much that I felt so loved and special. When things were good, they were amazingly good.

I loved my wife wholeheartedly, even though we reached the peak of our relationship in the first 2 to 3 years of our 11-year marriage. I loved her and longed for more of that which we had in the beginning. When things were good, they were amazingly good. She was a great lover, and I even wrote a couple of songs and poems about her. Hopefully, I will be able to publish them one day.

Song Titles: Something to me, Can I enjoy your eyes, You put a smile on my face.

Poem:

"As I look into her eyes, her smile, her glow, yeah, makes me feel alright. Makes me know she loves me, makes me want to shout out loud how I love her. That look of Love towards me makes me believe she's my everything, my everything, nothing I would do to capture that Look of Love again. From you, to see that look of Love in you. It's so lovely seeing the look of Love deep in your eyes".

She was smart, funny, and witty. She had the most amazing smile and the cutest dimples. She was savvy, creative, and well-spoken. Her voice is so sexy and sultry. Woo Hoo!!!

I captured this excerpt from a Facebook post concerning me. *Angelique Sep 14, 2013, • © Day 3- Today I am a happy wife because I was thinking of the times that my husband has told me," If I could give you the world, I would". Everyone enjoys receiving gifts, especially if they are lavish and*

She loved me at the beginning. She was sweet and engaging. Her attentiveness to me was wonderful. She spun her web around me, and I loved it. I didn't know that, like a light switch, she could turn things off as quickly as she could turn them on. I knew I had been had, but I was hooked and in Love. I was committed and determined to make it work.

As time went on, our exchanges waned, and all too many times, I found myself saying, "Come here, baby, let me kiss you," and it turned into "get away from me, don't you dare touch me!" After a few years of marriage, it is somewhat normal for a couple to squabble. It becomes a problem if arguments occur weekly, daily, or more often. When squabbling becomes a pattern played out all too often, frequent tension becomes the norm, and couples end up spending less intimate time together. They fall into the syndrome of being married and living as roommates rather than lovers. People stay in bad relationships. Many couples stay in a less-than-ideal relationship for various reasons. One blaring reason couples stay in a rocky relationship may be trying to save face, and so on. They may stay together for financial reasons, fear, familiarity, or even religious beliefs.

We had succumbed to the syndrome of being married and living more like roommates. Neither of us was unfaithful, neither of us uses or has a drug addiction or vices. However, we began to find many problems with one another, and one of us was strongly considering divorce. So, we began to go the way of many couples. We were going the way of senseless unhappiness (SU).

I must add that even though I'm writing this as a Christian, I realized that, regardless of religion, social, or economic background, senseless unhappiness happens on every level of relationships. Sad to say that professed Christian marriages have equal and sometimes worse failed marriages than non-Christian marriages.

Recent findings have revealed a startling statistic: almost 25% (and rising) of marriages within the Christian faith end in divorce. This stat comes from Longworth Law Fire, P.C. This number has risen significantly over the past few years, leaving religious communities around the globe concerned about the state of marital stability. While this figure may be disheartening, it does not mean there is no hope for couples who want their marriage to last a lifetime. With the proper steps and dedication, many Christian relationships can still find success in marriage.

While looking for reading materials on marriage at a Barnes & Noble bookstore, I was directed to the religious section. You asked why I mentioned this. It just seems strange to me that even a secular bookstore placed a book on marital help in the religious section. I am not certain, but many non-religious authors have written material on marriage. I guess subconsciously, they see marriage as a Godly institution.

I am fully aware that there are couples that experience verbal and physical abuse and infidelity addictions of all kinds, yet their marriage still does not end in divorce. Some stay in a less-than-ideal marriage, hoping that somehow things will change for the better. It is rare, but a few eventually enjoy blissful marital wholeness. The important thing is that you do something to sustain your marriage, other than just hoping things will get better.

Chapter 2
Foundational Instability

During our ceremony, we had the sand ritual. We selected married couples who demonstrated certain strengths, such as financial stability, spiritual longevity, and other areas. Every one of the couples we selected is still married (or has passed). Each of them still exemplifies the same strength that we admired and saw lived out by them. Each couple chose the color of sand that represented the strengths of their marriage. One vial of sand was poured upon the other. In theory, this was a great foundational principle for marriage, but unfortunately, we did not experience what the ritual emulated. It's not that it was unattainable; it's just that we never attained it.

Nevertheless, the foundation of God stands sure; he that builds his house upon a sure firm foundation (Matthew 7:24-27), no doubt it shall stand (2 Timothy 2:19-21). In hindsight, I recall that each couple we observed and chose for the sand ritual showed stability, strength, success, Love, and longevity. I can't help but wonder whether we would have gleaned many more priceless pearls of wisdom if we had gone to each of them for advice. We had all the tools and resources to achieve a beautiful, successful, and thriving marriage. Still, because we did not utilize those tools, we instead experienced the anguish and dismay of senseless unhappiness.

Dive deep, please, my friend. Please get your hands on as many marital help tools as you can. Resource ready, but more importantly, do whatever it takes, use all the tools you can to add stability to your marriage. (see workbook and references) Success is there right before your eyes. Find the joy and bliss you can regarding your marriage and be a beaming example to others. Show them that a beautiful marriage is achievable.

I recall my wife saying many times, "Marriage is work." On the contrary, if you don't work on the marriage properly, it will invariably not work well for you. You did run well, but what hindered you from obeying the truth? Galatians 5:7 I don't recall who it was, but it was a marriage counselor who said basically that when a marriage is going through trouble, one or both spouses behave selfishly and are centered on themselves, rather than on the marriage. I have listened to marital insights from many sound ministers over the years. To name a few, Pastor Rick Warren and Pastor David Jeremiah are Bible-based ministries.

How many marriages have the information to save it, yet never put into place the information that has been disseminated from them? The shame is that information doesn't save marriages; application of good marital practices does. Senseless unhappiness is the outcome more often than anything else.

There was a couple that we confided in who were not part of our ceremony, whose great Love and success in marriage I did glean from. The wife referred to her husband as her best friend. I also recall another couple we sought advice from and mediated our squabbling after listening to us, he replied and said, The things you're saying and doing towards one another." It is silly, and he put it bluntly and said, "Both of your attitudes suck. So, stop it." So sad, but neither of us was happy.

As I consider in hindsight, the focus of the sand ritual. Had we implemented the example we admired in each couple we chose. How much better our marriage would have been. The focus should have been on grabbing as much as we could from each couple and implementing their strengths into our own marriage. Many scriptures give sound advice and commands to strengthen marriage. For example: I Corinthians 13: Love is patient, kind, gentle... The greatest of these is Love... John 14:15 If you love me, keep my words (my sayings). Ephesians 5:25-33 Husband, love your wife. Give yourself to her. Sacrifice for her...Just as Christ gave Himself for the Church. You cannot pretend you can't see or understand His, namely Christ, example. Ephesians 5:21 says to love one another and submit to one another.

Win one another. Win at marriage, win the heart of your spouse again. Hold up the trophy high as you win. It might be great to have a trophy wife, but I guarantee you it's better to have a trophy marriage.

Rescue, Renew, Revive, Reconcile. God rescues souls; He can rescue a marriage. God can renew a heart; God can renew a marriage. God can revive (restore) a backslider back to Himself, then He can revive a marriage. God calls husbands and wives to be reconciled to each other as well. More importantly, God calls us to be reconciled to Him. 2Corinthians 5:18-19

In every story, there are three views (but only one truth): yours, theirs, and God's. I wish my late wife could give her side of the story. The memory of her I wish not to taint in any way in the eyes of those who knew her or those who never met her. I will continue to emphatically express that there's no argument to win nor side to take. My motive is purely to help others. My wife and I experienced some wonderfully blissful times together that I will forever cherish. My goal in sharing my story is simply to help others see that they don't have to remain in a senseless relationship, especially in marriage.

I want to let people know they are not the only ones experiencing trouble in Paradise. I put it this way, <u>"Paradise</u> <u>isn't owed to us, but it is</u> <u>achievable."</u> (yes, on this side of heaven). Please do all you can to avoid becoming a negative marital statistic. Praising your way through a particular thing satisfies you for a moment, but praying and praising your way through is what gets you through. The reality is that the problem still exists and has not changed. It occurs to you that you have no control over changing much of the situation. You're stuck in go-through mode. You've done all you know to move forward. As already alluded to, praising God gets the mind and outlook in a good place.

The process is not always up to the person or people who are going through it. SU The people who try to help are sometimes the same people who delay the process. You know that family member or bestie who always sides with you. The right people to help and resolve the situation may not yet be in place. The timing is of utmost importance. The parties involved have no control over when a resolution comes. However, that is when the sweet communion of the Holy Spirit is experienced. Once a testimony is established, it **becomes a tool and instrument that speaks to others who are still in their going-through process.**

Take the account of Israel wandering in the desert for 40 years. <u>Deuteronomy 1</u>: Our God Yehovah, because of the senselessness, hardheartedness, and stubbornness of the people. He saw their rebellion and decreed and declared that no one above a certain age would enter the Promised Land because of their disobedience. <u>(Deuteronomy 1:35-38)</u> The same goes for marriage; there's a place of promise to enter, unfortunately, or too many marriages fall short and die in the desert, never entering the fullness of what God has planned for the marriage.

At some point, in various situations, we experience and find that we are guilty of the same. Choosing, as did Israel, we must realise that it is our actions that tie God's hands. Often, the heartaches we endure leave us outside the purpose and plan that God has for us. As sad and sobering as this is, we must face the reality that some of the difficulties in our lives stem from our rebellion against God's commands.

Senseless unhappiness is like that sometimes; it just can't be understood *(Which I covered in chapter 1)* if you're in **<u>the going-through process</u>**. Go through, get through, but do so well with your mind, body, soul, and spirit. If you are responsible for bringing senseless unhappiness to your marriage or relationship, once you recognize it, repent and do something about it. Face it, take ownership, and say you're sorry to your spouse. Seriously, work on it. Do your part if you're the one contributing to senseless unhappiness. Let your spouse know and affirm your Love for them, but also let them know this is not the way to live. So, get to work and focus on what God has in store for your marriage. Peace and blessings to you.

Chapter 3
Dysfunction

Senseless unhappiness, periods of dysfunction, screaming matches, and the accusing merry-go-round of arguing about the same things repeatedly without any resolution became part of our lives. I share this not to shame myself or my late wife, but simply to describe the living conditions and the situation we went through.

Some of you readers may have experienced similar situations in your own marriages. There are often differences in how each person handles things, money, for example. One spouse may be good at saving, while the other is not. The funny thing is that what I labeled as dysfunction in her, I am certain she did not see as dysfunction at all.

Over time, I found myself focusing more on my own issues. Introspection became the first thing I turned to whenever problems arose between us.

Senseless unhappiness in marriages and relationships is coupled with personal traits, both good and bad, as well as upbringing. Relationship discussions about drama and baggage are very real and true, but can be very sensitive and difficult to unpack. There's good baggage and not-so-good baggage. They need to be dealt with from the source they stem from. Although it is often hard to understand the person you're married to, rest assured, they are not trying to harm or hurt you. They are the way they are because they know no other way, and at times, they may clam up and shut down under pressure. If you dare take the journey to peel back some of the layers behind their story carefully, you'll discover a better understanding of some things they struggle with. Making light of dysfunction never helps. It may take a long time to resolve some dysfunction, and it may take a professional to unravel its complexities. (The Mindful Marriage, Ron & Nan Deal)

My dysfunction was yelling, getting loud, and becoming extremely angry, hands flailing. I considered myself harmless, and I justified my actions as a way of expressing my frustration. My wife brought my behavior to my attention and let me know my actions were intimidating. I'm a big man standing 6'4", so when I'd get upset, it was quite frightening to her 5'5" frame. I'm certain it is the same for kids. I saw myself as a harmless teddy bear; they saw a **big ole bear.**

Parenting styles can have a significant impact on marriage, as can fiscal management or lack thereof, and the domestic approaches within a home. We, as individuals, revert to our upbringing without realizing it. The default mechanisms built into us, good and bad (see The Mindful Marriage). I discovered that there are dominant characteristics that emerge in a marriage, whether in parenting, finances, or education, which can affect a marriage both positively and negatively. My wife reminded me often of how critical and short my responses to our children were. In retrospect, they were more fearful of my reaction and response to them, causing them to withdraw from me. Even though I told myself I would never treat my children the way I was treated as a kid, being yelled at and not being heard. Instead, I repeated the same behavior, not realizing it was a built-in mechanism. It reared its ugly Head, affecting my children and my marriage negatively. [The Mindful Marriage Author describes this type of behavior as operating out of our pain cycle.]

From my first marriage came three boys whom my wife and I raised together. I was the dominant and strict parent. I showed affection to my boys and expressed Love toward them, which was the opposite of what I experienced growing up. In my own eyes, I believed I was doing a good job.

My then-wife, however, was very nurturing and soft-hearted as a parent. My complaint was that she did too much for the boys. Still, we both supported them in sports and were involved in their lives.

For a long time, I beat myself up, seeing myself as a bad father and wondering what I could have done differently. But when I ask myself honestly if I was there for them, the answer is yes. Their mom and I were there for them. They were raised in a Christian home. We provided for them, even though we didn't have much. Still, they were able to do many things I never had the chance to do as a child.

Again, I believed I was doing a good job because they had it better than I did.

Shortly after my second wife and I got married, we moved into a rental home. We did need the space, but the rent was far above what we could truly afford. That decision turned out to be the beginning of our financial struggles.

There were times when it was difficult to keep food on the table or even buy diapers for our daughter. I was not afraid to ask for help from food pantries or anywhere else we could find support.

No matter the circumstances, all the outcomes fell on my shoulders, both the good and the bad.

For a short time, my wife worked the second shift as a hotel attendant. We only had one working vehicle. When her shift was over, the kids and

I would get in the car and drive to pick her up. Sometimes, for convenience, she would just take the car instead.

Nothing in my wildest imagination prepared me to become a father again so late in life. My wife was more than five months pregnant before she even realized she was carrying a child.

I remember one Saturday morning when she asked me to feel her stomach. She believed what was happening in her belly was caused by fibroids. She scheduled an appointment with her primary physician, and that was when she discovered she was pregnant.

The night we went to the hospital, there were serious complications. Her OB/GYN was affiliated with a very small hospital, and they were not equipped to handle the trauma she was experiencing. The doctors said they would have to life-flight her to another hospital that had better facilities.

I had to drive there and meet her.

It was around four o'clock in the morning. Both her life and our child's life were in danger. My wife had to receive a blood transfusion and was given two pints of blood. Thank God she made it through that ordeal.

After nearly a week in the hospital because of the complications, I was finally able to bring them home.

It was Christmas Eve.

Chapter 4
The Unblended Blend.

Here I was, starting all over again with a new wife and two young boys. I had a second chance to get it right, yet I had no idea what battles lay ahead.

We talked about what those challenges might be. I remember telling her that as the boys grew older, there would likely come a time when they would push back against my place in their lives. I assured her that if we maintained a united front during those moments, things would work out.

Unfortunately, I later experienced the opposite. When things became difficult, she sometimes gave in; the children gained leverage, and I ended up losing ground. I had even warned her that if we failed to present a united front, I would end up being the fall guy.

My wife loved her children deeply through nurturing and encouragement. Later, I learned that she did not believe in physical discipline, punishment, or what she described as negative actions or talk. It quickly became clear, rightly so, that I lacked patience. I also realized that encouragement was not one of my strongest skills.

Even so, I believed I had a better handle on things than the way I was raised. But the changes I made were not enough. At the time, I didn't recognize it, but now I see clearly that there was a serious imbalance in our approach.

I never envisioned the intense arguments we would have. I never imagined the impact those arguments would have on the little people living in our home.

Slowly, we began to grow farther apart. Blended-family challenges surfaced, and a spiral of discontent became our new normal. A new baby, job struggles, financial pressures, and on top of everything else, my own health issues weighed heavily on us.

Ugly arguments followed. Regrettable, bitter words began to choke the very life out of our marriage.

During our premarital counseling, we were given an exercise: outline a five-year vision for our future. I remember saying that the boys would be doing well in sports and academics. My wife would be playing her piano, filling the atmosphere of our home with music.

It was my intention and plan to share my writing with my wife. I truly believed we would co-write and tell our story together. In my mind, we would have ended up sharing a wonderful testimony of how God touched and healed our marriage. Such an outcome is what I longed for. I also believed we would have reached a place of wholeness in marriage. I implore you, before one of you dies or your marriage dies, please do not live senselessly, please do not live unhappily, please do not live without achieving what God has ordained for your marriage. Jeremiah 29:11 Do you have a healthy outlet to deal with the SU in your marriage? If not, do your marriage justice, reach out, and do something other than nothing.

I used to say to myself, "I just don't understand." I finally came up with the catchphrase, "because it can't be understood." Even with an understanding, it must be followed up with proper corresponding action.

Senseless unhappiness was a part of our children's world, also. It is almost impossible to put toothpaste back in the tube once it is squeezed out. Neither my wife nor I could ever undo the trauma we caused our children. I can still hear my daughter crying and saying, "Daddy, stop, don't be mad at Mommy." She did not care what we argued about; she just wanted it to stop. Each of the children responded differently; one tried to intervene, while another said nothing, stuffing it down.

Open disclosure of secrets and past experiences is important in a marriage. Intentionally holding back parts of one's past often comes from preconceived notions, either positive or negative. When things are withheld, it can leave room for conjecture about the reasons why.

Speculation about such behavior can run deep within relationships. When two people come together in marriage, the relationship can become complex, not because one spouse is trying to hurt the other, but because they often do not realize how their past issues have shaped who they are.

By the fifth year of our marriage, we had both lost our mothers. It was a strange and difficult time.

When her mother became ill, we traveled to New York to visit her. During that trip, I met her extended family. Later that same year, we returned to New York after her mother passed away.

That same year, I experienced the loss of one of my sisters to cancer, and by the year's end, my mother also passed away. In addition, I lost a woman who had been like a mother figure to me throughout my childhood. I mention her because I wanted to bring my daughter with me to Cleveland to attend her home going service. That choice became a significant source of conflict between my wife and me.

We clashed terribly over child-rearing issues. Looking back, I do not understand why we did not draw closer to each other during that season of loss. Instead, we walked through our grief in an eerily cold and distant way.

Senseless unhappiness affects everyone in a home—even those outside of it. Friends often feel forced to pick sides, which only makes matters worse.

Please take a long, honest look at how senseless unhappiness may be affecting your entire family. Stop and reflect. Repent to each person individually and collectively. Then go to Father God and repent.

Seek forgiveness from God and from one another.

Chapter 5
Who She Was

Both inwardly and outwardly, I saw my wife as someone who had it all together, intellectually and otherwise. She excelled professionally and was recognized as the top agent at the insurance company where she worked.

She was gifted, called, and flowed in an undeniable connection with women as she ministered to them. Women often sought her out for counsel, encouragement, and advice. There were countless times when I saw ladies looking to her while wiping tears from their eyes as she comforted them.

She was effective both in one-on-one settings and in group ministry. There were more prayer calls that she led than I can count. I witnessed the trepidation and anguish she experienced as she prepared for each T-Time event she hosted, as well as for the speaking engagements she was invited to participate in.

I watched my wife, Angelique, grow spiritually in prayer and dedication to the Lord. Over the eleven short years of our marriage, she developed into an anointed, powerful, and gifted minister of the gospel.

Before our marriage, she had never operated in ministry at any level, aside from playing the piano in her younger years for various churches when prompted by her late mother. Angelique was always reluctant to refer to herself as a minister or preacher. She preferred to elevate others rather than herself. It took her quite some time to openly acknowledge the call of God on her life.

She was a fervent prayer warrior and intercessor. She freely supported other women leaders, often using her talents in marketing, organization, and many other practical skills to help their ministries flourish.

There was clear growth and visible fruit in her ministry.

Below are testimonials from a few women who were impacted by her life and ministry.

Testimonial

"Angelique met me when I was only 19 years old. The Lord put it on her heart to come up to me and hug me. After that moment, I felt a strong pull to get to know her.

She quickly became a mentor to me, but she became more than just a mentor—she became a mother figure in my life.

She taught me how to follow the leading of the Holy Spirit. She also taught me how to pray with anointing oil and how to pray over people.

She was very Spirit-led, and she taught me to always be ready for the Lord—whether He was moving in the Church or if He was ready to call you home."

— Sarah S.

When I think of Angelique, I immediately think of her selflessness and the warmth of her hugs. She was more than a mentor in my life, and I thank God for strategically hand-picking her to disciple me.

Mom was a woman of dignity and honor, and her reverence for the Lord was contagious. I never knew what it was like to be a daughter loved by a mother until she came into my life.

She was Holy Spirit–led and understood the importance of discipleship. She knew how to correct me out of Love and called out the good in me. She always called me "beloved" and saw me as God saw me, not through the pain I had endured.

The wisdom she imparted to me I will forever hold close to my heart. She was a prayer warrior, and there was never a time that I can recall when I did not see her pray.

There are not enough words to express the impact she had on my life. She was always a woman of strategy, and if there is one thing she often told me, it was, "You have to be quick on your feet."

Because of her, I am a better mother, and I have come to understand the value of who I am as a woman and how precious my worth truly is.

— Kierra M.

Angelique took her assignment here on this earth seriously and left behind a legacy that will forever be unmatched. She led with gentleness, yet there was incredible strength behind it.

What an honor it was to have her in my life, and I will forever be thankful. To know her was to love her, and she truly was a gift from God.

I first met Angelique shortly before her wedding to Ron. At that time, I did not know her well. I knew Ron, who was part of our ministry. Over time, I watched her grow into a very powerful woman of God.

I saw how God used her in our prison and jail ministry. I witnessed how God birthed her own ministry, T-Time, which stood for Transformation. I watched her pour into the lives of women, young and old alike.

It was an honor to have her in my life during the few short years we spent ministering together. Though our time together was brief, she was obedient to the Lord Jesus and faithfully walked out the call of God on her life.

— Ruth B.

Sitting at a Tim Hortons in the Hilltop area of West Columbus, Ohio, would be the last time Angelique and I shared face-to-face fellowship. I considered her a dear friend and sister.

Her Love and passion to see hurting women delivered were demonstrated at every women's T-Time gathering and conference she hosted.

Angelique was a gifted and professional businesswoman who did not mind getting "dirty" for Jesus. She was always willing to let Jesus Christ work through her, and yes, to love through her hugs.

Angelique was deeply committed to her relationship with the Lord. This precious woman of God had a heart that longed to see hurting, wounded, battered, and bruised women healed.

It didn't matter what a woman looked like, whether she appeared unkempt or well put together. Angelique would become the hands and feet of Jesus, lifting women up and surrounding them with the Love of God.

Matthew 25:35-36 (NKJV), "For I was hungry, and you gave Me food; I was thirsty, and you gave Me drink; I was a stranger, and you took Me in; I was naked, and you clothed Me; I was sick, and you visited Me; I was in prison, and you came to Me."

— Evangelist Sharon H.

Angelique was a gift I never knew I needed. She was the one who helped me fall in Love with the Lord in a deeper and more personal way. In every season of uncertainty, every question, every fear, every doubt, she was the safe place I could run to. I trusted her with my heart because she carried truth with tenderness, honesty with grace. She protected me, warned me when others didn't have my best interest at heart, and covered me in prayer when I didn't even know how to pray for myself. She believed in the purpose God placed inside me, even in moments when I couldn't see it. She spoke life into me, pushed me closer to God, and never let me forget who I was in Him. Her presence, her wisdom, and her Love changed my walk forever. I will always carry her in my heart, grateful that God allowed our paths to cross.

— Holly M.

My wife Angelique wrote a short devotional for women. Her family, including her brothers and sister, was not aware of the level of involvement their sister operated in as a minister. At her homegoing, a video clip of her in action was shared. Her sister commented that she had no idea that "Angie" (the name her siblings called her) was involved in ministry, as the video shown let alone that her sister had written a devotional. There was a side to her that she did not let me in on. I knew she lost her dad at the age of seven. I knew she lost her twin brother in her late teens or early twenties. She told me she lost him to cancer. I found out later that he died from something else. I know her first marriage ended due to abuse to the point where her life and her first son were in danger. To say the least, she experienced trauma in her life.

Chapter 6
Our last day together

Death ultimately caused her, and us, to part ways by means neither of us saw coming. One Sunday at Church, Angelique filled an entire row with people who meant so much to her: her spiritual daughters and a couple of spiritual sons. There was a young woman present who had not attended Church in over a year, yet after Church, Angelique spent the final afternoon of her life ministering to her. Afterward, she came home that evening. Neither of us realized she was living out the last hours of her life.

My wife was on the phone planning her next Women's Meeting. I kissed her good night and retired to bed. I heard a loud thud, which I ignored, thinking it was weights dropped by my son. The lady my wife was on call with called me and asked me to check on Angelique and my daughter, who was in the den. I did as she suggested. I called out her name several times, but there was no response. Eventually, I had to force my way into the bathroom where she was. She lay unresponsively on the floor; her Head wedged in the corner. I frantically fumbled to dial 911. During the phone call with the 911 operator, I was instructed to check her breathing. I did not detect any breathing.

Once the EMT paramedics arrived, they instructed me to leave the room and to take the children upstairs while they tried to revive my wife. Later, one of the paramedics called me down to let me know they were going to transport my wife to the hospital. The same paramedic told me they could not get a pulse from my wife. We all got in the car to meet them at the hospital. Shortly after our arrival, to our dismay, she was pronounced dead.

When two people come together in marriage, the relationship can become so complex, not because the spouse is trying to hurt the other, but because they don't realize how their issues have affected those close to them. As I mentioned in Chapter 3, peeling back layers of our past sheds light on our personalities, our upbringing, and so forth. Try to consider this when you encounter a challenging situation in your relationship with your spouse. The more layers you peel back, the more that's revealed. The more you open up to one another, the more it can challenge and help your marriage.

The enemy of our souls attacks and fights hard to destroy the family unit. It's hard to fathom why she and I had so much trouble in our marriage. I came from many years of ministry service and looked forward to her and me working side by side in that same capacity. I envisioned us operating as a powerful, flourishing husband and wife ministry team in the Kingdom of God. At some point, I honestly believed we would become a powerful ministry couple. Unfortunately, that never came to fruition. I, along with my stepsons and our daughter, was numb and shocked by her sudden passing.

Who's to say how much trauma, loss, and difficulties in one's life affect their marital relationship, but it's evident that it does, and each person handles it differently. (The Mindful Marriage). Emotional manipulation and control!!! Losing self or natural inclinations.

The thing is, as I write, I think about the things that were left unsaid, my inner thoughts that she never heard. There are some things that she never told me, not because of hiding something. It is just because you don't always get to speak your complete mind. This book allows me to share some of those thoughts.

A Side Note on Perspective

The stress and anxiety caused by the turmoil in our marriage had a direct impact on both my wife's health and my own. For her, Atherosclerotic Cardiovascular Disease (ASCVD) ultimately claimed her life. Neither of us knew how severe her condition had become.

As for me, I was a ticking time bomb—one explosion away from death. About six months to a year after my wife passed, I faced serious health challenges myself. I cannot fully explain how I survived. I know that I could have been gone, but by the grace of God, I am still here to tell the story of how His sure mercies carried me through.

I will never understand why I survived and she did not.

Of course, I cannot say with certainty that the stress from our marital struggles directly caused our health problems, but I am quite sure it did not help. Our poor diet also contributed to the issues we faced.

I have gone through significant health challenges, but thank God, I am now on the other side of them. I am beginning new chapters in my life. Recently, I obtained a license to sell life insurance and am moving forward with a renewed sense of purpose.

Testimony of a Successful Marriage

Many people enter marriage seeking perfect Love, but God often uses marriage to perfect our Love.

Marriage is not about finding the right person, it is about becoming the right person. It is not about being served; it is about serving.

There is truly no such thing as a perfect marriage, but being married to your best friend can make the journey much easier.

Every marriage is different. My husband became my best friend because of the respect and care he showed me. In the same way, I became his best friend through the respect and Love I showed him.

We loved spending quality time together and taking care of one another. Our Love and companionship deepened as we faced the many trials and hardships of life together.

I strongly believe that our marriage lasted so long because we both loved and served the Lord for fifty years. We endured dangerous toils and snares because we centered our lives and our marriage around the Word of God.

Through obedience and instruction, we surrendered to Jesus. We had conflicts. Oh yeah, absolutely, but we were always able to resolve any conflict through prayer and talking things out.

— Ruth B

The aftermath of divorce: abandonment, fallout for spouses, children, family members, friends, leaves behind a trail of betrayal. The impact can be devastating on those it affects. In their reactions, they blame animosity, unforgiveness, hurt, pain, Betrayal, jealousy, and envy. Most, if not all, come from rebellion and disobedience.

Expecting a person to fulfil what only God can fulfil is unrealistic. Your expectations more than likely will not be met by your spouse. Like social media, where good, nice, and beautiful posts appear, isn't a true depiction of that person's life, but rather a snapshot clip of their reality. Unmet expectations (identify them, find out the source, and reason them out. Unrealistic expectations (get rid of them)

Via my disobedience in both my marriages. Caused me to wander in the wilderness, not entering the promises of God for my family and me. There is a chance, though slim. For all there remains a rest according to Hebrews 4:1-4. These verses speak concerning the Sabbath's rest and the children of Israel entering the promised land. It also speaks of those who did not enter the rest, the land of promise

We must bear in mind the origin of marriage, as it was created and established by God. Had we taken this fact to heart. I can only imagine how much better our marriage would have been. Looking back at my marriage, it was good, except for the arguments, lack of respect, financial difficulties, differing opinions concerning child rearing, and lack of intimacy. As I examine these, I notice that respect and intimacy are deliberate choices. The other things were communication and circumstance instances. For example, you can choose to disrespect, or you can choose to respect. You can choose to show your spouse intimacy. You are the one who can meet your spouse's intimate needs. While disagreements can sometimes be resolved through counseling and improved communication, financial problems are frequently due to circumstances. Good goal setting and right planning, education, opportunities, fortitude, and sometimes chance affect outcomes. It is so sad that we missed enjoying one another all too many times over the years!

Can you learn from unpleasant experiences? Based on my experience, I answer an emphatic yes. Angelique and I were both active and committed to our Church. We both participated in homeless and jail ministry. I was also part of a drama Ministry. I became consumed with my troubled marriage, which affected me in ministry.

Chapter 7
My Healing

Men are rarely vulnerable in their relationships. I often wondered who would even want to hear my story, especially when it is messy and imperfect. Throughout my struggles, journaling became a form of therapy for me—a way to make sense of what I was going through.

Along the way, I encountered others who quietly shared similar marital unrest. What struck me was how much of it remained on the surface. Most people hold back, afraid of what others might think if they reveal too much. Society tends to prefer stories of victory rather than honest accounts of hardship, pain, and even defeat.

In time, I forgave her, and I forgave myself for my part in our unhappiness. Our struggles were not one-sided; we were both unhappy. Today, I find myself better, not bitter. I remember battling feelings of bitterness and anger toward my spouse, but I also recall rebuking and rejecting those thoughts. My prayers became more intentional, focused on healing and restoration.

It is often said that we learn from our troubles and failures. But when hope fades, and there is no obvious triumph, no one wants to hear about it, let alone talk about it. As a result, many people suffer in silence, carrying their pain alone.

Counselors and therapists often encourage openness and honesty, but that is not always easy. There is certainly a time and place to focus on the positive, yet sometimes we must bring our darkness into the light, just as Scripture teaches. Only then can what is hidden be exposed, so true healing can begin.

Take, for example, someone who has suffered a deep wrong, such as sexual assault. Too often, the victim remains silent to avoid shame or humiliation. It takes enormous courage to share such pain, knowing it may lead to judgment or even rejection. Some people may applaud that bravery, while others may criticize it or suggest the story should have remained private.

Even those who have found redemption after failure may never again be seen in a positive light by some. We are often told not to complain because no one wants to hear it. But I believe that sharing our stories, even when they are painful or unresolved, can bring hope and healing, not only to ourselves but also to others who may be suffering in silence.

The Challenge of Vulnerability

Sometimes sharing the full extent of our struggles feels like "too much information." When we experience hardship, society often responds with a dismissive attitude, suggesting we should simply get over it, toughen up, and move on.

We are told, directly or indirectly, to deal with our pain alone and to keep quiet about it, as if speaking openly about our struggles were a sign of weakness.

In my own experience, even those closest to me have warned that opening up too much could change the way others see me. There is pressure to stay within the boundaries others have set for us—to remain inside the box people believe we belong in.

That expectation can make it even harder to be honest about our pain or to allow others to see the less polished parts of our story and our lives.

Marriage, as established by God, remains unchanged. He has not altered His design for marriage since its inception. Scripture tells us that God hates divorce, yet at one point, He divorced Israel. In Jeremiah 3:8, this act is presented as a metaphor. God divorced Israel because of their idolatry and unfaithfulness.

God requires submission to His authority, and there are consequences for rebellion and disobedience. Yet even in the midst of judgment, God's redemptive plan remains.

Paradise still exists. The Tree of Life still exists. Every believer in Christ has a guaranteed invitation to the Marriage Supper of the Lamb, a celebration that will last for all eternity.

The connection between marriage and the ultimate Paradise in heaven is profound. Revelation 19:7–9 speaks of the Marriage Supper of the Lamb, while Revelation 21 describes the new heaven and the new earth. In that restored creation, the Tree of Life appears again, its leaves bringing healing to the nations.

When humanity was driven from the Garden of Eden, the way back to the Tree of Life was guarded by an angel and a flaming sword (Genesis 3:24). Paradise was not destroyed; it was preserved. Though humanity experienced trouble in Paradise and fell into sin, redemption through Christ ultimately restores what was lost. The curse is reversed, and access to the Tree of Life is restored.

Ultimately, every redeemed believer in Christ will share in this eternal promise.

While reflecting on these truths, I came across a prayer I once prayed and sent to my wife. Although that prayer was never fully realized within my own marriage, I now pray it for couples who still hold on to the hope and promise that only God can fulfil.

A Husband's Prayer

My wife and I prayed for you this morning—not only for you, but for ourselves. I asked our Father, yours and mine, to remove the facades and false images that the enemy has painted.

I asked God the Father to remove the distorted images placed before us by the enemy—images that do not reflect who our Father created us to be.

Our Father revealed to me that the enemy has whispered things into our ears that contradict the vows we spoke to one another before people and, even more importantly, the vows we made before our Heavenly Father.

He showed me that many lies have been spoken that oppose the truth God has ordained. It is a lie that our union was a mistake or that we are incompatible.

Just like a scene in a movie or a play filled with props and dramatic music, the enemy creates illusions to make us believe his version of reality. But the drama he portrays is not the reality God intended for us.

We must proclaim what Abba has spoken over us. We must renounce every lie the enemy has used to haunt us.

It is time to kick over the enemy's props and stand firmly in the truth that God the Father has spoken over us and the vows we made before His holy presence.

We can no longer allow what the devil has devised and scripted to replace what our Father has written about us in His Holy Word.

My wife and I prayed for us in the Spirit. I heard far more than I could write.

There is freedom in this. I remember seeing how close we were to victory, and it was not far away.

— Author Unknown

Over time, I have read many books and resources about marriage. I was pleasantly surprised to discover that there are numerous sound and helpful materials available. I have gathered excerpts that are both practical and encouraging.

I strongly encourage couples to seek as much wisdom and insight as possible to help keep their marriages healthy and strong.

Kay Yerkovich, a respected marriage therapist, offers valuable insights on this subject, and I would like to share one of her resources with you.

Kay Yerkovich is a licensed marriage and family therapist specializing in treating couples, with attachment theory serving as the foundation of her work. She is a popular speaker and lecturer in the areas of parenting and marriage relationships, and she supervises and trains other therapists. Kay and her husband, Milan, are co-authors of the books "How We Love " and "How We Love Our Kids." The couple has four children and several grandchildren. Learn more about Kay and her work by visiting her website:

www.howwelove.com.
https://relationship180.com/love-styles/.

For a few of us, our early childhood experiences and love lessons were ideal, and our love style was healthy and positive. Most of us, though, have had hurtful experiences resulting in a harmful imprint and impaired love style, and that can handicap our marriage relationship.

Naturally, we all want to feel we are doing our best as spouses. To do our best, we must take an honest look at what hinders us. Keep in mind that the goal is not to find fault with our parents. The goal is to acknowledge the truth of our childhood, so we have a road map for growth and change.

5 unhealthy love styles

1. The avoider
2. The pleaser
3. The vacillator
4. The controller
5. The victim

Pastor Les's exposer happens both ways. Things that are in you become revealed. Reconciliation: To make a relationship work, it takes two willing; not to make it work only takes one not willing. It's not important to win the argument, but diffuse it and address it again at another time. There are times you must forgive.

My own choices led to career financial indecision and missed opportunities. I did not plan, so as the saying goes, "I had planned to fail. Until now, in my sixties, I have not had any financial planning tools in place in my life. Throughout my entire adult life, financial planning and savings have been something I will get around to one day.

In my first marriage, which lasted twenty-five years, I walked away to pursue my own selfish desires. As a result, I ended up in an unhappy marriage; the proverbial grass was not greener on the other side. I repented to God.

Blame is not the focus at all, nor is it badgering oneself, but instead learning the application of Godly principles and examining our selfish motives, making corrections as revealed by the Holy Spirit. Perfect, none of us are. Life comes with enough hardship on its own; it's part of our human existence. The joy of the Lord is (truly) our strength. Happiness along the way is (truly) a bonus to us physically, financially, mentally, and spiritually.

Do not recklessly live your life. Harness success and live it out. Manage your outcomes, cultivate and treat every aspect of your life as the precious asset that it is. Do not miss all life has to offer. One life, one body that encompasses the duration of your existence. Do it well, live it well, live it intentionally.

Strive to maintain healthy relationships throughout the affairs of your being. Choose with purpose to have a 'why' wherever possible. Avoid reckless and destructive behavior, as well as risk-taking.

The success of a good marriage. Control yourself instead of manipulating your spouse. Know how to behave. Train yourself to obey.

The purpose of writing SU: Of a certainty, we all have a past we bring into a relationship. Individuals vary in how they manage experiences from their past. Awareness of these can help a couple both independently and collectively. Such awareness provides a focal point for addressing issues in a healthy way. I hope that something within the pages I have written will point towards addressing and resolving some issues positively.

Chapter 8
What Is Love? - Dr Myles Munroe

Love alone is not enough for a successful marriage. Love can be deceiving and may not be a reliable foundation for marriage. While Love can bring happiness, it does not necessarily provide the tools and skills needed to make a marriage work.

A successful marriage requires knowledge and understanding of how to live with and commit to your partner. Learning how to navigate the challenges of a committed relationship is a crucial element of building a lasting and fulfilling partnership.

Love can make us believe that we can overcome any obstacle in a relationship. However, the reality is that many divorced individuals were once deeply in Love with their partners. This challenges the idea that Love alone is what keeps a marriage together.

While Love can bring happiness, it does not contain all the ingredients necessary to sustain a marriage. Knowledge is what truly helps a marriage grow and succeed.

Many people enter marriage based solely on their feelings of Love, without considering the practical realities and challenges of sharing life with another person. Our culture often places a strong emphasis on emotions, which can lead people to make commitments impulsively without fully considering the responsibilities of a long-term relationship.

To protect and sustain a marriage, individuals must gain knowledge about how to navigate the complexities of a committed partnership.

This includes understanding effective communication, conflict resolution, compromise, and the ability to adapt to change. When couples develop these skills, they are better equipped to build and maintain a successful marriage.

In conclusion, Love is not the only factor that determines a successful marriage. Knowledge about how to navigate the complexities of a committed relationship is essential for building a lasting and fulfilling partnership.

#thedeepthings #wealthmindset #DrMylesMunroe #family #love

Dr. Myles Munroe, *The Purpose and Power of Love and Marriage* (2005)

The following are some ways to approach finding the answers that are necessary:

1. Fix it and make it work, create a workable plan.
2. Find out why the problem exists and address it directly.
3. Take note, adjust, customize, and execute.

I say this because, in the aftermath of my marriage, we often submitted to our own opinions rather than to Scripture. Much heartache could have been avoided. Recently, I heard teachings about principles and facts that do not change when it comes to God's Word. One of those facts is that God's Word is my authority. Jesus is my authority.

Since this book is about marriage, I wonder how many discussions couples have had about differences in opinion concerning submission, headship, and spiritual authority, to name a few.

Our reasons for not submitting and obeying are many. Often, we decide that these teachings are outdated, archaic, wrong, or that they have a different meaning for our time. Few people actually read the biblical instructions on these subjects. If they have read them, some choose to ignore them. We may believe they are conditional, open to interpretation, or culturally outdated.

We get into trouble when we modify the design. The fearful, the cowardly, the timid, the reluctant, the disobedient, the rebellious, the doubters, and the unbelievers must all come to obedience in Jesus Christ. The alternative, according to Scripture, is final judgment and banishment (James 3:13–15; Revelation 21:8).

Next comes the workbook section, which offers a practical and workable plan. Let's dive in and begin. The goal is to align our lives with the design and will of our Creator. Take note, adjust, customize, and execute.

A word must also be said about abuse and ungodly authority. Scripture reminds us that justice ultimately belongs to God: "Vengeance is mine; I will repay," says the Lord (Romans 12:19). God also said to Cain, "The voice of your brother's blood cries out to Me from the ground" (Genesis 4:10). There have always been tyrannical leaders, unreasonable and demeaning bosses, and abusive husbands. If your life is ever endangered, flee from such situations. With the authority that God has delegated to men comes the responsibility and accountability before God.

Find ways to revive and rekindle your exchanges with one another. Thoughtful planning, deep reflection, and careful consideration can help restore connection in a relationship. Take time to meditate on what your spouse means to you. Find a poem that best expresses your sentiments toward your mate. Write a letter, a note, or a card, and give it to them.

I wrote the following letter to my wife during a time when she was feeling discouraged. I cannot recall the exact situation now, but the words remain meaningful.

My wife, please see that your husband is here for you, even when it may seem otherwise.

My arms are here to hold you.
My lips are yours to kiss and to speak blessings to you and over you.
My eyes are here to behold you, to receive your invitation, and to draw nearer.
My ears are open to listen and hear your requests, even those I may not be able to fulfill.
My hands are yours to hold and embrace in whatever way you need.
My feet are swift to come to your rescue or to stand beside you.
My heart is yours, to be filled with your Love, joy, and peace.

My wife and I speak these words of encouragement to you. As a co-laborer in our Lord's service, as my sister in the Lord, as the mother of our children, and as my friend, you may say that you did not ask for the ministry of the Lord. But the moment you said yes to the assignment, you accepted it.

The Lord knew you would say yes. That is why He equipped you and gifted you to carry out that assignment. He also knew the frustrations, obstacles, and trials you would face along the way.

More importantly, He knew that you would not fail to give Him the glory, honor, and praise for every triumph and victory that would come through your obedience to His call on your life. I remind you of the lives that are being changed, strengthened, and encouraged because you chose to obey and say yes.

You are not alone. He is at the helm of your ship. Rouse the Master and let Him speak to your storm. Let Him speak to you, His daughter. Ask the Father, Daddy Abba, to calm you, His child. Ask Him to speak peace to the waves and the winds. They must obey, just as you have obeyed.

Yes, let His peace settle gently over you now.

Holy Spirit, do it for her in this very moment. Hallelujah.

Lastly, I wrote the following words in frustration during a difficult season in our marriage:

Kiss you? I can't.
Touch you? I can't.
Hold you? I can't.
Look at me.
Talk to me.
Listen to me.
Lay with me? I won't.
Trust me? You don't.
Be with me? You won't.
Love me? I won't. I can't. I don't.

If you find that your marriage is stuck in any of these places, stop right now and seek help. Take the hand of your spouse, repent before God, and pray together. The verses provided in this workbook can guide you.

If you are reading this alone, go to your spouse lovingly and sincerely. Take them by the hand and begin with prayer. Speak honestly and gently as the Holy Spirit leads you. Do not remain stuck where you are.

Take heart in the institution of marriage, which came from God. Marriage reflects a return to the paradise where the first couple once lived in harmony with one another and with their Creator. As you continue through this workbook, we will explore the foundational Scriptures that reveal God's design for marriage and provide the biblical support for restoring and strengthening it.

Chapter 9
Insight

Over the years of my marital ups and downs, I have learned a great deal. I am often surprised by the truths that have unfolded, dare I say, revealed themselves to me. While finishing this book, God gave me insights that I know came only through the Holy Spirit. The spiritual keys discussed in this section are one example.

We will begin by understanding the hierarchy of spiritual authority.

Finding your way amid the fight and the struggle requires a decision: choose to explore the institution of marriage as God designed it. Take this journey together.

Keys to YHWH's Design for Marriage

1. Submission
2. Cleaving
3. Unity (Helpmate), oneness, "bone of my bone" (while recognizing that enmity may have slipped into the relationship)
4. Nakedness
5. Rule and Headship
6. Desire
7. Nourish and Cherish

When used properly, these keys unlock doors and provide access to tools and principles that strengthen and fortify your marriage.

Do you trust your King?

Do you honor and respect the one you married?

If your answer is no to either of these questions, then prayer and careful examination are necessary. Ask God to correct whatever is misaligned in your heart.

If you do not surrender in submission as God has instructed, you place yourself at a disadvantage. Those who refuse to use the master key of submission remain locked out of what lies behind the door of God's design for their marriage.

You cannot gain access if you never use the key of submission—that is, spiritual authority—to unlock what is behind the door. Fear often stops us and freezes our momentum. To truly understand submission, we must first understand the spiritual authority that God has established.

1. Submission

This key represents trust, obedience, and humility. Scripture calls believers to obey and to be in subjection to one another (Ephesians 5:21–22). Submission acknowledges and respects the order that God has established.

You might ask, "Why should I submit?" The answer is simple: because it is the order that God (YHWH) has chosen. There is order and design in everything our Creator has made.

2 Cleave

This key opens the bond of unity between husband and wife. Scripture tells us that a man shall leave his father and mother and cleave to his wife, and the two shall become one flesh (Genesis 2:24). Jesus reaffirmed this truth, saying, "What God has joined together, let no one separate" (Matthew 19:6; Mark 10:9).

It is also noteworthy that enmity was placed between the seed of the woman and the serpent (Genesis 3:15). Some argue that there is a greater conflict between man and woman, but Scripture clearly places that enmity between humanity and the serpent, not between husband and wife.

3 Helpmate

This key fosters compatibility, servanthood, and oneness. Scripture says, "And the Lord God said, It is not good that the man should be alone; I will make him a help meet for him" (Genesis 2:18).

A helpmate helps and is suitable, complementary, and opposite in design. God created the woman to stand alongside the man as a partner. When the woman was brought to the man, he declared her to be "bone of my bone and flesh of my flesh." This declaration emphasized unity and partnership. The man was instructed to cleave to his wife, and together they would become one (Genesis 2:23–24).

4 Nakedness

This key unlocks the beauty of intimacy within marriage. In the beginning, the man and the woman were naked and unashamed (Genesis 2:25). Their nakedness represented openness, vulnerability, and complete trust.

From a marital perspective, intimacy should not be approached with shame. In the garden, the husband and wife lived together openly and without embarrassment. Within the covenant of marriage, husbands and wives should feel free to share themselves fully with one another.

Shame, insecurity, and neglect of self-care can negatively affect the marriage bed. Scripture reminds us that marriage should be honored and kept pure (Hebrews 13:4). Within marriage, intimacy is meant to be a gift, not a source of shame.

5 Headship and Leadership

This key is twofold, unlocking both responsibility and trust. First, it involves accepting the role of leadership and responsibility that God has delegated. Second, it involves trust and cooperation within the marriage relationship.

Scripture teaches that "the husband is the head of the wife, even as Christ is the head of the church" (Ephesians 5:23). Likewise, "the head of every man is Christ; the head of the woman is the man; and the head of Christ is God" (1 Corinthians 11:3).

Leadership in marriage is not domination but responsibility. To rule means to guide, protect, and govern with care. When a husband leads with wisdom, humility, and Love, his wife will feel safe and willing to support and follow that leadership.

Just as not all believers fully submit to Christ as the Head of the Church, not all wives submit to their husbands. At the same time, a husband's leadership can be hindered when unity and trust are lacking. Marriage functions best when both partners work together in harmony.

6 Desire

This key unlocks passion and emotional connection within marriage. Scripture notes that the woman's desire will be for her husband (Genesis 3:16). This speaks to longing, closeness, and the deep emotional bond between husband and wife.

Intimacy within marriage involves more than physical connection. It includes affection, emotional support, and a deep desire for one another. The husband and wife should seek to listen to one another's voice above all others. Outside influences that attempt to create division should not be allowed to disrupt the unity of the marriage.

Again, Scripture reminds us that the true enmity established in Genesis 3:15 is between the serpent and the seed of the woman, not between husband and wife.

7 Nourish and Cherish

This key opens the door to agape love, the sacrificial Love described in 1 Corinthians 13.

Husbands are instructed to love their wives as Christ loves the Church (Ephesians 5:25). Scripture also teaches that a husband should love his wife as he loves his own body (Ephesians 5:28–29). Just as a person cares for their own body, a husband is called to nourish and cherish his wife.

To nourish means to provide care, encouragement, and spiritual support. To cherish means to protect, value, and hold dear.

Ephesians 5:26–27 also speaks of sanctifying and cleansing through the Word. This reflects the husband's responsibility to support his wife spiritually and to cultivate a home where God's Word guides their lives.

Just as Adam was originally charged with tending and keeping the garden, husbands are called to care for and protect their wives with Love, patience, and devotion.

Verse-by-verse scripture references for marriage.

Genesis 2:15, 3:23-25, Romans 13:1-4, Ephesians 5:23-26, 28-29,31,33, Ephesians 4:15-26, 5:23-33 1Corinthians 7:3-5, 1Corinthians 11:3, 11:7-12, Hebrews 13:7, 1Peter 3:1-7 , Revelations 21:2(9) the bride of Christ

The fallout: Banishment

1. From heaven, the serpent is not satisfied with the one he wants to destroy, both man and woman, thus the marriage.
2. From the garden, one another, heaven, the very presence of God.
3. From community, Satan is not satisfied with the one; he wants the family. (Cain and Able). Bruising the heel of the seed of the woman, guarding, having his Head crushed. Banished by the Beguiling Serpent, Mind infiltration other than contrary thoughts, Questioning, of God's authority-leadership, knowing good and evil, meaning ramifications.??? Consequences of immaturity, lies, the lies, the lies.

Before and after the fall

Before there was good, after there was good and evil,

Before there was dominion, after there was rule submission,

Before there was Innocence, after their immaturity,

Before, there was nakedness without shame; after, there was shame and covering,

Before there was access, after there was expulsion,

Before there was security, after there was fear,

Before there was trust, after there was mistrust, confusion, and doubt.

Before there was openness, after there was hiding, submitting, and commitment come first, love often follows. Love is not guaranteed that couples will remain in love, let alone committed & submitted. While being committed and submitting can lead to love. Falling in love is not the key, but loving one another is the key.

Chapter 10
Biblical Covering

The first mention of "covering" in the Bible is in Genesis 3:21, where God makes coats of animal skins to cover Adam and Eve after they realize their nakedness and try to cover themselves with fig leaves. This divine provision signifies God's grace and foreshadows the ultimate covering for sin, while Adam and Eve's makeshift fig leaves represent inadequate human attempts to hide their shame.

Genesis 3:21 (NIV): "The Lord God made garments of skin for Adam and his wife and clothed them."

Context:

- Human Attempt: After eating the forbidden fruit, Adam and Eve sewed fig leaves together to cover themselves, but these were insufficient and temporary.
- Divine Provision: God then intervenes, providing more durable coverings made from animal skins, which required the sacrifice of animals (shedding of blood) to create.
- Symbolic Meaning: This act is seen as the first instance of substitutionary atonement, where an innocent life (the animal) covers the sin of the guilty (humanity), pointing to Jesus Christ as the ultimate covering for sin.

In some Christian circles, discussions about "covering" often extend to the idea of being under the authority of a pastor or spiritual leader. However, when examining the scriptures, I do not find direct support for the notion that "covering" specifically refers to pastors or spiritual leaders. Instead, this concept appears to have developed more from tradition or adaptation than from explicit biblical teaching. Nevertheless, the Bible clearly establishes pastors and leaders, assigning them specific roles and responsibilities within the framework of spiritual authority as defined by Scripture.

In 1 Corinthians 11:7-12, Paul discusses the significance of head coverings, emphasizing that a man should not cover his Head because he reflects the image and glory of God. In contrast, women are described as the glory of man, highlighting the distinct roles and representations of men and women according to biblical teaching.

The passage states: "A man ought not to cover his Head, since he is the image and glory of God; but woman is the glory of man. For man did not come from woman, but woman from man; neither was man created for woman, but woman for man". The culture of that day was that a certain covering worn by a woman identified her as a submissive wife to a husband. Paul then clarifies that, in the Lord, men and women are interdependent, just as woman came from man, so also man is born of woman, and everything ultimately comes from God.

The reference to "because of the angels" in verse 10 suggests a deeper spiritual order or hierarchy. Some interpretations connect this to Genesis 6, where fallen angels interacted with humans, leading to consequences for both. The idea is that spiritual beings observe human conduct, especially in worship, and that proper order and symbols of authority are important in the presence of the divine and the angels.

The story of Mary, the mother of Jesus, illustrates submission to God's will. When the angel told Mary she would bear the Son of God, she responded in faith: "Let it be to me according to your word." This demonstrates the importance of yielding to God's plan and authority.

These passages are challenging and often debated, but by focusing on the cultural context and the specific words, order, image, tradition, headship, covering, glory, authority, and angels, we see a clear outline of hierarchy: God is the Head of Christ, Christ is the Head of man, and man is the Head of woman. The Head of every man is Christ.

- The Head of Christ is God.
- The Head of a woman is a man.
- A woman came from a man.
- A woman was created for man.
- The Head of every man is Christ.

To clarify, 1 Corinthians 11:10 emphasizes that a woman should have a sign of authority on her Head, which is especially important "because of the angels." This phrase points to the spiritual order and hierarchy that God has established. Instead of getting caught up in debates about what this symbol specifically means, it's helpful to focus on the broader message: God has created a structure for relationships and worship that reflects order and respect for divine authority. The mention of angels suggests that spiritual beings observe human actions, particularly during prayer, and that maintaining proper conduct is significant in their presence. Genesis 6, where fallen angels interact with humanity, highlights the consequences of disregarding God's order. According to Genesis 6, the interaction between fallen angels and humanity led to widespread corruption and violence throughout the earth. You can also explore Hebrews Chapters 1 and 2, which discuss the role of angels. Angelic interactions with man gave man help and instruction concerning the order and will of God.

Rebellion and Submission:

Ephesians 5:15-16 "But speaking the truth in love, may grow up into him in all things, which is the head, even Christ: From whom the whole body fitly joined together and compacted by that which every joint supplies, according to the effectual working in the measure of every part, maketh increase of the body unto the edifying of itself in love."

Not all men love their wives as Christ loves the Church (or themselves). Make the decision to explore God's design for the institution of marriage together.

Submission comes by way of obedience to headship, which leads to Cleaving, which leads to vulnerability and trust, which leads to Honor and Love of one another.

Some insight on rebellion: 1 Samuel 15:23 Rebellion (submission) is as the sin of witchcraft. Satan sought power, lusted after Envy, and desired to be worshipped. Have you ever thought or said, "I'll submit when? (fill in the blank) Satan rebelled and was kicked out of heaven. Adam disobeyed and got kicked out of Eden. Cain disobeyed and then committed murder. As a result, he was banished and labeled a vagabond.

Is it rebellion, disobedience, or mistrust against God? Those who rebel and refuse to repent are banished. Commit murder, kill. What are you banished from? (hell) Misery Heaven Eden paradise Family relationships Society The fallout from your own rebellion. Are you the cause of your failing marriage by way of rebellion?

When we rebel, it is perpetrated by people, most often those closest to us. For Cain, it was his brother he lashed out against.

Killing his brother did not fix his disobedience to God.

It's the same for the rebellious wife against her husband, the rebellious child against parents, the rebel worker against his boss; ultimately, it's against God that we rebel.

The first rebellion was directly against God. All rebellion derives from the first and original rebellion.

We labeled those over us as unfit, incompetent to rule or govern us There will always be those who argue and stew and steam about inequality and injustice, equality. Unfortunately, all too many miss out on God's design. He is the only Head who controls all. The man is next in control. God blesses the marriage through submission.

He blesses the man and the woman as they submit together to God's authority (headship given to her husband) and hierarchy that He has put into place.

God gave man dominion over the works of His hands.

Who is man that you are mindful of him, or the son of man, Psalms 8:4, Hebrews 2:6-9

There are expectations we have and assumptions we make concerning marriage. We assume the person we marry has the same depth of understanding of scripture that we have. I dare to say that most of us have not done a complete study of what the Bible teaches concerning marriage.

It's time take a walk through the Bible concerning marriage, explore individually and collectively before marriage, and continue referring to it during marriage. Prayerfully study and reflect on what God says in the scriptures concerning marriage.

Write down your understanding. Were there mindsets you needed to align and realign?

Write them down. Discuss and pray with your spouse about your insights. Repent as needed, as God, Holy Spirit, to give you understanding.

What are some takeaways concerning the scripture keys?

Write down your takeaways and refer to them as a reminder.

"Respect, value, listen." The prayer of Jabez 1Chronicles 4:9 &10 . That part where he prays, I pray no harm come to me. Have you ever done anyone harm, unintentionally or intentionally? I ask you specifically when it comes to your mate. Would they say that you have done them wrong? Have you labeled them as painful to you? Are you the harm that they need to be kept from?

What are you doubting concerning your marriage? What do you wrestle with? Why do you have what you have? Why don't you have what you want? What do you need to do to get what you want?

Who has what you believe you want?

Do you have a clear visual of what you want?

Submission understands what God intended.

Enmity (fight right) against, as opposed to awareness!

Naked and unashamed (clothed) Headship/subject Love self-focused or otherwise Nourish and cherish (sentimental care) endearment) Obedience to Christ versus disobedience. Depriving one another (tend to the needs of your mate)

Honor (esteem) Covering (clothing garment) Order and rankings (Awareness hierarchy)

The rule head governs over (wife, you are a subject of your marital kingdom) as a good King husband rules well, then will your subject love and want to submit to you.

Wife- Desire long for stretch out for your husband, versus the opposite (the whisper of an enemy is to come between), the only whisper you hear (give voice to) should come from your mate. {note control can be abused and mismanaged} trust him who is in control...

Desire to longing \ Ruled over Process the meaning through prayer, seeking the meaning and purpose. Flawed thinking could very easily cause things to go awry. What words, phrases, and reasoning lies have you yielded to? Man was given dominion before Eve was created.

Divide the divorce. Longing Desire/rule of the woman and her desire for her husband (Alone/not good), resolve woman created for the man, Bone of bone, flesh of flesh, Innocence, shame.

Workbook Description

This workbook is a practical, faith-based guide designed to help couples reflect, communicate, and take actionable steps toward healing and strengthening their marriage. Drawing from the author's personal testimony and years of ministry experience, this book offers honest insights into the realities of marital struggles, including "senseless unhappiness," foundational instability, and the challenges of blended families. The workbook combines introspective questions, exercises, and biblical principles to foster growth, reconciliation, and deeper connection.

Readers will find relatable stories, spiritual wisdom, and practical tools for navigating conflict, rebuilding intimacy, and understanding the spiritual authority within marriage. Each section encourages couples to examine their relationship, communicate openly, and apply scriptural truths to everyday challenges. The workbook is interactive, featuring exercises for independent reflection and joint discussion, making it suitable for couples at any stage, whether facing a crisis, seeking renewal, or simply wanting to strengthen their bond.

With references to respected marriage resources and biblical teachings, this workbook is not just a companion to the author's story, but a roadmap for couples who desire lasting change and marital bliss as designed by God. It is ideal for those who have considered separation, experienced divorce, or feel stuck in their relationship, offering hope, encouragement, and practical steps toward restoration.

Workbook Description For Marriage Counselors

This workbook is a comprehensive, faith-based resource designed to support marriage counselors in guiding couples through the complexities of marital challenges. Drawing from the author's personal journey and decades of ministry, it provides a candid look at the realities of "senseless unhappiness," foundational instability, blended family dynamics, and the spiritual dimensions of marriage.

Structured with introspective exercises, discussion prompts, and biblical principles, the workbook equips counselors with practical tools to foster honest communication, emotional healing, and spiritual growth. Each section encourages couples to reflect independently and together, facilitating deeper understanding and reconciliation. The workbook's interactive format allows counselors to customize sessions, address specific issues such as conflict resolution, intimacy, and unmet expectations, and track progress over time.

Key features include:

- Introspective exercises for individual and joint reflection Faith-based guidance rooted in scripture and spiritual authority
- Real-life scenarios and testimonies to normalize marital struggles
- Actionable steps for restoring connection, trust, and intimacy
- References for respected marriage resources for further support

Ideal for use in counseling sessions, workshops, or group settings, this workbook empowers counselors to help couples move beyond surface-level solutions and address the root causes of marital distress. It is especially valuable for couples considering separation, recovering from divorce, or seeking to renew their commitment. By integrating spiritual wisdom with practical strategies, marriage counselors can facilitate lasting transformation and help couples achieve the marital harmony and fulfillment designed by God.

Workbook Section

For husbands and wives

Exercises to be completed independently of one another for introspection:

Please take time to pray together as you work on the exercises:

The validity of one another's responses must be respected; please don't downplay in any way. You both need the freedom to express how you feel. Heartfelt communication and natural exchanges. That leads to your well-being as a couple.

Exercise #1: How I see us

My wife/husband is very aware of how I am doing most of the time (true or false express by percentages), ex, 10% - 100%

____

____

I am attentive to the needs of my wife/husband. (list them) (their health or yours, for example)

____

____

____

I am guilty of ignoring my wife/husband.

____

____

Why have I not connected to my wife/husband lately?

____

____

How have I connected with my wife/husband lately?

____

____

How intimate have I been with my mate in the past few weeks?

____

____

How has my mate felt about our interactions lately?

____

____

What has been the primary focus of your conversations with your mate as of late?

____

____

To what extent have you been directing your attention towards your spouse as compared to yourself recently?

____

____

Graph your interaction with your spouse. What does it look like? About money, travel, retirement, etc.:

Ex. Highs, lows, spikes, peaks, flats, dips. If each positive interaction were equivalent to cash, how rich or poor would your relationship be? Credit yourself for $100 with every positive response.

____

____

How does your mate know when you desire intimacy?

____

____

Do you give verbal hints, or do either of you say exactly what you want?

____

____

Do you often feel ignored, taken for granted, unwanted, and despised?

____

____

If you were to rate your level of meeting your mate's intimate needs based on percentages, what would that be? Emotionally, physically, mentally, spiritually, socially

____

____

____

____

Exercise #2 Exchange and presence

Based on your recent exchanges with your spouse, which of these applies to you?

Are you available and present or checked out and disengaged?

____

____

Do you say more than you do? Faith without Works is dead:

____

____

____

____

Is your marriage stagnating?

____

____

Do you dismiss your mate before you hear them out?

____

____

Do you welcome or put off the advances of your spouse?

____

____

Is their receptivity or reciprocation when advances are made?

____

____

Are you tenacious or do you just give up amid the rejection in the moment?

____

____

Do you want to be touched, kissed and embraced?

____

____

Exercise #3: What I want her/him to know

Ladies, Men ask yourselves, what do you want to say to your wife/husband should you precede them in death?

____

____

What do you want to share with them for the rest of your lives collectively?

____

____

Write it out for them to read now or later. Write a letter for both instances.

What do you want for your mate that they don't already have?

____

____

What is it that you dream you would like to see fulfilled for them?

My husband/wife would say I'm very _______________ about? _______________ (fill in the blanks)

My husband/wife would love it if I would

____

____

The Reconciliation of US! To settle a quarrel, bring back into harmony. Sharps, flats, and pitchy-ness. Put it to rest!!! Reconciliation: properly, be of one voice (voice the same opinion); bilateral agreement between marriage partners to temporarily abstain from sexual relations, (used only in 1 Corinthians 7:5). Sharps, flats, and pitchiness

Exercise #4 Discontentment

What is your quarrel about?

____

____

Can you point out the problem?

____

____

Serve it up, what are some of your relationships (DNA, i.e., dynamics)? Ex: traits; Word of caution here, please do not badger one another concerning their response. Allow for grace if their answers are short or long. Do not get nervous if they take too long or even if their response is too quick.

____

____

____

____

What caused you to fall for her/him? (write them a minimum of 3 things)

____

____

____

Examples for me: her wit, intellect, laugh, and affection towards me, her way of commanding my attention, empathy, compassion, past hurts, disappointments. Her Love and devotion for Christ! Our Camaraderie banter exchange subtly subtleness.

Find ways to revive and rekindle your exchanges with one another.

Forethought planning, deep thinking, and Meditation consideration. Find a poem that best speaks your sentiments to your mate. Write a letter, a note, and a card, and give them to them!

I wrote the following letter to my wife during a time she was feeling less than. I wish I could recall the situation; however, here it is.

My wife, please see that your husband is here for you. However, it may seem the contrary. My arms are here to hold you. My lips are yours to kiss, to speak blessing to you and over you. My eyes to behold you, to receive your invitation, to draw nearer. My ears are open to listen to and hear your request, even those I cannot meet. My hands are yours to hold and embrace anyway you need. My feet are swift to come to your rescue or stand beside you. My heart is yours to be filled with your love, joy, and peace!!! My wife and I speak these words of encouragement to you. As a co-laborer in our Lord's service, as my sister in the Lord, as the mother of our children, as your friend, you did not ask, you say, for the ministry of the Lord. Oh, but you did the moment you said yes to the assignment. The Lord knew you would say yes, which is why He equipped you and gifted you to conduct that assignment. He also knew the frustrations, obstacles, and trials you would have to face.

More importantly, he knew you would not fail to give Him the glory, honor, and praise for every triumph and victory that came because of your obedience to His call on your life. I remind you of the lives that are being changed, strengthened, and encouraged by your obeying and saying yes.

You are not alone. He is at the helm of your ship. Rouse the Master, let Him speak to your storm, let Him speak to you, His daughter. Ask the Father (daddy-Abba) to calm you, His child. Ask Him to speak peace to the waves and the winds, they must obey as you have obeyed!!! Yes, let His peace brood and settle over you now... Holy Spirit, do it for her this moment, Alleluia!!!!!!!!

Exercise #5: State of my marriage

What is the current state of your marriage?

____

____

Things between us are consistently inconsistent, awkward, and unnatural. What steps have you taken to change or correct?

____

____

Are you still attracted to each other, purposeful gaze into one another's eyes?

____

____

No natural effort to touch (Physically, emotionally, spiritually). Write out your responses independently of one another.

____

____

____

____

"A good Marriage is the closest thing to heaven on earth that there is."

Let me explain, when a marriage is a good one, people recognize it. A good marriage gives the unmarried an example to follow. Children emulate and cause them all to be envious of them. A good marriage makes for a better community and thus a better world.

The prayer of Jabez. 1 Chronicles 4:9-10 That part where he prays, I pray no harm come to me. Have you ever done anyone harm, unintentionally or intentionally? I ask you specifically when it comes to your mate. Would they say that you have done them wrong? Have you labeled them as painful to you? Are you the danger they should avoid?

Verbally, physically, jealously using harsh, cutting words. Belittling, emasculating, bashing them, tearing them down.

Have you done so privately around your children or others? Those types of actions cause pain; in such cases, repentance is very much in order. Certain behaviors we expect from an enemy. David reminds us in Psalms, "the enemy that wounded me or came from a friend, someone close. Someone of my equal. My companion and my acquaintance. Psalms 55:12For it is not an enemy who reproaches me; Then I could bear it. Nor is it one who hates me who has exalted himself against me; Then I could hide from him. 13But it was you, a man my equal, my companion, and my acquaintance. We took sweet counsel together and walked to the house of God in the throng.

Exercise #6: What kind of spouse am I?

Are you your husband's wife? Explain

____

____

____

Are you your wife's husband? Explain

____

____

____

Are you married indeed or just on paper?

____

____

____

Do you have a biblical marriage? If your answer is no, then why not? (Refer to scriptures shared in Chapter #8 for the next three responses)

____

____

____

If your answer is yes, present evidence?

____

____

____

____

"I don't have to be right. Being right is not the goal! Arriving at the same goal together is the destination" Control yourself instead of controlling your mate, adjust your behavior to behave. Train yourself to obey

Bonus Material

I would be remiss if I did not address the biblical teaching on the covenant. Scripture describes marriage as a covenant in several passages, often, unfortunately, highlighting instances where people failed to honor their promises. For example, Proverbs 2:17 speaks of an adulteress who "has left the partner of her youth and ignored the covenant she made before God." In Malachi 2:14, God expresses His displeasure, declaring, "because the Lord is acting as the witness between you and the wife of your youth, because you have broken faith with her, though she is your partner, the wife of your marriage covenant." Similarly, in Ezekiel 16:8, God uses covenant language to describe His relationship with Israel: "I gave you my solemn oath and entered into a covenant with you, declares the Sovereign Lord, and you became mine."

First and foremost, marriage as a covenant signifies a lifelong commitment to one another. The marriage bond is only dissolved by the death of a spouse or if one partner willfully abandons their vows in a profoundly destructive way.

Second, understanding marriage as a covenant means recognizing that God alone can sustain a marriage, especially during the most difficult seasons. There may be times when commitment to Christ is the only thing holding a couple together, when emotions fade, when external pressures mount, or when other motivations fall short. In those moments, it is the promise made before God that endures. Psalm 15:4 praises the one who "keeps his oath even when it hurts." Faithful men and women who follow Christ are those who honor their promises.

Third, the covenant of marriage means that, under the lordship of Jesus Christ, the husband-wife relationship becomes the primary human relationship in your life. This covenant calls Christians to put their spouse first, above parents, friends, children, and even personal passions or pursuits.

The Washing

As Christ loves and cares for his church, so should men love their wives

Wash her with the Word!

Read scripture to her, speak the Word over, pray with her

Adorn, clothe her, engage her, bathe her with the Word of God

Be the Priest of your home, minister to Adoni (The Lord), and gain His instruction

Minister to her as instructed, then to your family and others

Present her (put her on display)

Love your wife as Christ loves the Church (as you love yourself)

Sacrifice for her as Christ sacrificed for the Body

Cherish and nurture her

Sanctify and cleanse her, wash her with the water of The Word (Ephesians 5:26), submit and commit.

1. Cleave be subtle physically, be close to her with intent. Go on a walk together. Be in the room with her on purpose. (in other words, be present) Let her know you notice a fragrance she wears and compliment her on how you like how she smells. Shop for a fragrance you like, take

notice of her clothing, and tell her what you like her to wear. Hold her hand, touch her more often, be intentional.

2. Give her sincere, honest compliments when around others. Make efforts to freshen up your look, shave more often, pay closer attention to yourself, and don't go into debt, but treat yourself to something new. Then purposely parade yourself in front of your wife. Check with someone at the clothing store, thumbs up or down. If you take better care of yourself, be sure to take care of her.

3. Go out of the way to give her something she has her heart set on doing or having. Pay attention to sacrificing your wants with priority over your needs.

4. Nourish and cherish, feed her naturally and spiritually.
Do so with warmth and affection.

5. Sharing a scripture verse or a teaching gives some insight and words of encouragement to her. Remember being intentional. Simply read passages of scripture to her.

6. Remind her of your commitment to her, to your marriage, and to God.

7. Tell her what you adore about her womanhood. For example: the sound of her voice, her hair, her soft skin, her tenderness

Tell her how you love being her hero, getting rid of a bug, or retrieving an item out of reach. Fixing something broken in the house.

As a young boy, I recall my mother teaching me how to use the old wringer-style washing machine and how to hang clothes on the clothesline to dry. She even taught me how to use a washboard. God has instructed the man how to wash and care for his wife in His Word. His son Jesus has washed us with the Word. He said, "I have washed you, but not all of you are clean; be cleansed by washing the regeneration and renewing of the Holy Spirit" Titus 3:4-6. Be skilled with the Word, the blood of Jesus has washed our sins away. The Word of God continually keeps us clean.

Become skilled, be trained and instructed in the Word of God. Don't defer to her to lead your home spiritually, especially if you have children in the home. Train young children and young adults in the hierarchy of marriage as designed by God YHWH.

<u>Be exemplary to the young and premarital.</u>

I asked my 12-year-old daughter out of curiosity. What do you think you should look for in your future husband? I shared a scripture with her out of Ephesians about how the wife is to obey her husband. The look on her face was priceless. She said, <u>"Obey. Am I a dog?"</u> Her response was one of rejection of this notion of obeying. I asked her a question. Do you feel like you are a dog if you obey the Lord? She said Well, no, I said so. Why would you feel like you're a dog? If you obey your husband, I further explained to her that a wife obeys her husband as she obeys the Lord. She nodded her head like Oh. And it dawned on me that even young children need to be taught how to submit to obeying God's design for marriage. Upon thinking about this further, I realize that most children go to school for 12 years, some go to college for another four years, and even others go on to get a master's degree or a doctorate, and I begin to think that we train our children and prepare them for academics. They grow up and get married, and most marriages last 10-20, even 30 years or more, but we do nothing to train or prepare our children for marriage. It's so funny that we spend a good portion of our lives focusing on getting married without any formal training. The conversation needs to be had with young children, let alone adults, about what marriage is in the eyes of God. Maybe this approach could help people avoid troublesome marriages.

A wedding is narrowed down to a day, a ceremony, and half an hour or so. A marriage is to last a lifetime. We plan for a wedding as an event. We should prepare for marriage. We recite vows and design vows that we prefer. We fail to consider that vows are not the foundation of marriage. There is a reason we ought to spend much more time preparing and training children according to a scriptural marriage.

Ancient Jewish weddings were a series of events that took place over a week:

- Betrothal: The groom's father would negotiate a price with the bride's father, and the couple would sign a contract and drink wine.
- Waiting: The groom would return to his father's house to build the bridal chamber.
- Consummation: The groom would return to the bride's house at night to bring her to the bridal chamber and consummate the marriage.
- Wedding: The bride would be brought into the groom's home in a colorful procession.
- Feast: The wedding guests would feast and celebrate for seven days.

In ancient times, marriage was considered a purchase, and betrothal was the most important event. However, as women became more important and marriage became less of a purchase, the wedding became more important.

Today, Jewish wedding ceremonies are usually between 20 and 30 minutes long. After the ceremony, the couple and their guests celebrate with a festive meal and then continue to celebrate with friends and family for seven days.

The engagement period lasted a year.

The marriage of the Lamb has, and His bride has made herself ready...as a bride adorned for her husband (2nd time)

John 14: ... I go to prepare a place

Matthew 25:6 ... the bridegroom comes; go out to meet him (fanfare) it's a thing...

Mark 13:32-37... watch, pray, you don't know the hour that the good man comes

Revelation 21:2 A bride adorned for her husband; prepared, made ready (ready getting ready) ... for her husband

Revelation 21:9... come, I'm going to show you the bride, the lamb's wife (those written in in the Lamb's book of life), the bridal party procession, the reception venue

Lamb's book of life (guest book) Luke 14. An eternal celebration. Traditionally, a Jewish wedding feast lasted 7 days.

Two-Week Marriage Devotional

Daily Reflections for Growing in Unity, Love, and Faith

Week 1: Foundations of Godly Marriage

Day 1: Submission and Authority

Read: Romans 13:1-5, Hebrews 13:17

Reflect on God's design for leadership and submission within marriage. Pray for humility and a spirit of cooperation as you each seek to honor God's order.

The converse of: Rebellion, disobedience, pride, modify,

Day 2: Cleaving to One Another

Read: Genesis 2:24, Ephesians 5:31

Consider what it means to leave and cleave. Discuss ways you can prioritize your relationship above all others.

The opposite is: Disunity annul, separation, division, single independent.

Day 3: Oneness in Christ

Read: Ephesians 5:23-26, 1 Corinthians 12:12

Meditate on unity and oneness as the body of Christ. Pray for God to deepen your spiritual and emotional intimacy.

Day 4: Nakedness Without Shame

Read: Genesis 2:25, Ephesians 4:15-26

Reflect on vulnerability and honesty in marriage. Commit to open communication and emotional transparency.

Day 5: Rule and Headship

Read: Ephesians 5:23-29, 1 Corinthians 11:3

Discuss biblical headship and loving leadership. Explore ways to support and encourage each other's strengths.

Day 6: Desire and Cherishing

Read: Genesis 3:16, Ephesians 5:28-29

Reflect on God's call to cherish and nourish one another. Pray for renewed affection and desire in your marriage.

Day 7: Unity Despite Conflict

Read: Ephesians 4:26, 1 Corinthians 7:5

Talk about healthy ways to resolve disagreements. Ask God for grace to forgive and restore unity when conflict arises.

Week 2: Growing in Love and Purpose

Day 8: The Bride of Christ

Read: Revelation 21:2, 9

Reflect on your marriage as a reflection of Christ's love for His Church. Renew your commitment to love sacrificially.

Day 9: Submission and Respect

Read: Ephesians 5:33, Hebrews 13:7

Consider the role of respect and submission in marriage. Pray for hearts that honor and uplift one another.

Day 10: Nourishing Each Other

Read: Ephesians 5:29, Genesis 2:15

Discuss practical ways to care for and nourish each other daily, both spiritually and emotionally.

Day 11: Cherishing the Union

Read: Ephesians 5:28-29, 33

Celebrate the gift of your union. Write down things you cherish about your spouse and share them.

Day 12: Standing Against Enmity

Read: Genesis 3:23-25, 1 Peter 3:1-7

Pray for wisdom to recognize and resist anything that threatens your unity. Ask God to help you stand together in faith.

Day 13: Mutual Help and Support

Read: Genesis 2:18, Ephesians 4:15-16

Reflect on being a helpmate. Look for new ways to encourage and serve each other in daily life.

Day 14: Lasting Commitment

Read: 1 Corinthians 11:7-12, Revelation 21:2

End with prayer, asking God to continue strengthening your marriage as you walk together in submission, unity, and love.

This is an extensive list of scripture, including definitions:

Marriage is honorable and the bed undefiled. Hebrews 13:4 1Corinthians 7:5 defrauding not one another... Do not withhold intimacy from your mate or be intimate with someone other than your mate.

"Defraud **650** *aposteréō* (from 575 */apó*, "away from" and 4732 */stereóō*, "deprive") – properly, keep *away* from someone, i.e., by *defrauding*(depriving); to cheat, taking away what rightfully belongs to someone else. ye not one the other, except it be with consent for a time, that ye may give yourselves to fasting and prayer; and come together again, that Satan tempt you not for your incontinency." Want of power, intemperance (in a wide sense), lack of restraint. **192** *akrasía* (from 1 */A* "not and 2904 */krátos*, "prevail") – properly, without prevailing (taking dominion), i.e. the inability to maintain control; (figuratively) without self-control and hence mastered by personal appetites (urges).

1 Corinthians 7:5 "Let the husband render unto the wife due benevolence: kindness; euphemistically, conjugal duty -- benevolence, goodwill. good-will, kindliness; enthusiasm.; euphemistically, conjugal duty -- benevolence, good will. good-will, kindliness; enthusiasm."

1 Corinthians 7:3 "But he that is married care for the things that are of the world, how he may please his wife; but she that is married care for the things of the world, how she may please her husband." 1 Corinthians 7:33-34

Ephesians 5:23 "For the husband is the head of the wife, even as Christ is the head of the church: and he is the savior of the body. Therefore, as the church is subject unto Christ, so let the wives be to their own husbands in everything. Husbands, love your wives, even as Christ also loved the church, and gave himself for it; That he might sanctify and cleanse it with the washing of water by the word, so ought men to love their wives as their own bodies. He loves his wife, loves himself. For no man ever yet hated his own flesh; but nourishes and cherishes it, even as the Lord the church: For this cause shall a man leave his father and mother, and shall be joined unto his wife, and they two shall be one flesh. Nevertheless, let every one of you love his wife even as himself; and the wife see that she reverences her husband. Ephesians 5:23-26, 28-29, 31, 33

1 Peter 3:6 "Even as Sara obeyed Abraham, calling him lord: whose daughters ye are, if ye do well, and are not afraid with any amazement."

Genesis 18:12 "Therefore Sarah laughed within herself, saying, After I am waxed old shall I have pleasure, my lord being old also?"

Lord, husbands (1), Lord (5), lord (172), lord's (9), lords (2), master (91), master's (24), masters (5), owner (1). "And the Lord God said, It is not good that the man should be alone; I will make him an help meet for him." Helpmate: **Azer help, suitable; opposite**

Our obedience to God first comes from our love and submission to God as Father, then to his word (law). "Unto the woman he said, I will greatly multiply thy sorrow and thy conception; in sorrow thou shalt bring forth children. **and thy desire shall be to thy husband, and he shall rule over you**."

Genesis 3:16 desire: in the original sense of stretching out after; a longing -- desire. Rule: dominion (1), gain control (1), govern (1), had charge (1), have authority (1), master (1), obtain dominion (1), really going to rule (1), rule (27), ruled (5), ruler (18), ruler's (2), rulers (6), rules (9), ruling (3), wielded (1).

1 Peter 3:1, 5-7 KJV "Likewise, ye wives, be in subjection to your own husbands; that, if any obey not the word, they also may without the word be won by the conversation of the wives.

For after this manner in the old time the **holy women also, who trusted in God, adorned themselves, being in subjection unto their o**wn husbands: Even as Sara obeyed Abraham, calling him lord: whose daughters ye are, if ye **do well, and are not afraid with any amazement**. Likewise, ye husbands, dwell with them according to knowledge, giving honor unto the wife, as unto the weaker vessel, and as **being heirs together of the grace of life**; that your prayers be not hindered."

Subjection:

Submission: to place or rank under, to subject, mid. to obey **Usage:** I remember under, subject to; mid, pass: I submit, put myself into subjection. "Rule and desire" (sorrow at the time of conception)

Genesis 3:16 "Unto the woman he said, I will greatly multiply thy sorrow and thy conception; in sorrow thou shalt bring forth children; and thy desire shall be to thy husband, and he shall rule over you."

Your desire shall be to your husband, and he shall rule over you. God gave man dominion, Gen 3:28 2;19&20 Adam Named Woman his wife after the fall [Sorrow in and at conception] Knowing [awareness of good evil] saw it was good for food Pleasant to the eyes desire to make wise

Definition: of evil? After transgression (Transformation, transgender), we commit to the spiritual process in which we are changed through the power of God.

Transgression: when we go contrary to the will and obedience of God. Trans??? Leave a natural process and process it into something away from its natural state or form.

1)Their eyes were open (saw that which they had not) [better off never knowing a thing or something] naked awareness (which they had always been) [exception now they saw themselves differently]

2) They hid (felt differently) toward God

3) Afraid, who told you you were naked? Questions??? What have you done? Reasonings, excuses, and blame followed!!! Consequences given and carried out. The voice of God, the voice of the serpent, the voice of the woman (Adam's wife). What voice are you listening to?

Ephesians 4:15-16 "But speaking the truth in love, may grow up into him in all things, which is the head, even Christ: From whom the whole body fitly joined together and compacted by that which every joint supplies, according to the effectual working in the measure of every part, maketh increase of the body unto the edifying of itself in love." Grow up in the head, grow up in love, which is Christ! Fitly joined. The body is compacted together, supplied by every joint according to the effective working measured to all parts, which makes and causes the body to edify and build itself in love.

As blood is to the human body, Love is to the body of Christ!!! 1 Corinthians 11:3 "But I would have you know that the head of every man is Christ; and the head of the woman is the man; and the head of Christ is God."

1 Corinthians 12:12 "For as the body is one, and hath many members, and all the members of that one body, being many, are one body: so also, is Christ." As the body of Christ is fitly compacted, joined together effectually working, so should be the marriage of the believer.

"And whatsoever ye do in word or deed, do all in the name of the Lord Jesus, giving thanks to God and the Father by him. Wives, submit yourselves unto your own husbands, as in the Lord. Husbands, love your wives, and be not bitter against them." Colossians 3:17-19